VITAMINS AND MINERALS

BY DR. ALVIN SILVERSTEIN, VIRGINIA SILVERSTEIN, AND ROBERT SILVERSTEIN

ILLUSTRATIONS BY ANNE CANEVARI GREEN
FOOD POWER!
THE MILLBROOK PRESS ■ BROOKFIELD, CONNECTICUT

Library of Congress Cataloging-in-Publication Data

Silverstein, Alvin.
Vitamins and minerals / by Alvin, Virginia, and Robert Silverstein
: illustrations by Anne Canevari Green.

p.   cm.—(Food power!)
Includes bibliographical references and index.
Summary: Examines the major vitamins and minerals, their
functions, sources, proper daily dosages, and deficiency symptoms.
ISBN 1-56294-206-9 (lib. bdg.)
1. Vitamins in human nutrition—Juvenile literature.   2. Minerals
in human nutrition—Juvenile literature.   [1. Vitamins.
2. Minerals.   3. Nutrition.]   I. Silverstein, Virginia B.
II. Silverstein, Robert.   III. Green, Anne Canevari, ill.
IV. Title.   V. Series: Silverstein, Alvin. Food power!
QP771.S56   1992
612.3'99—dc20   91-41231   CIP   AC

CONTENTS

Your Body Is Just Like a Factory **5**

The Micronutrients **6**

What Are Vitamins? **8**

The Vitamin Pioneers **14**

What Are Minerals? **16**

Vitamins and Minerals
for Good Health **22**

Water: The Forgotten Nutrient **28**

The Two Groups of Vitamins **30**

Minerals: Major and Minor **36**

Nutritional Values of
Common Foods **42**

Glossary **44**

For Further Reading **46**

Index **47**

YOUR BODY IS JUST LIKE A FACTORY

① **FOOD** IS THE **FUEL** THAT KEEPS YOUR FACTORY RUNNING.

② THE FACTORY USES MANY THINGS IN FOOD: **CARBOHYDRATES**, **FATS**, **PROTEINS**, **VITAMINS**, **MINERALS**, AND **WATER** (WHICH HELPS COOL THE FACTORY AND CARRY THINGS AROUND IT).

③ **CARBOHYDRATES** (SUGARS AND STARCHES) ARE THE FURNACE — THEY PROVIDE ENERGY.

④ **FATS** ARE THE STORAGE DEPARTMENT: THEY STORE ENERGY FROM FOOD AND ALSO CARRY VITAMINS AROUND THE FACTORY.

⑤ **PROTEINS** ARE THE BUILDING BLOCKS THAT ARE USED TO REPAIR AND ENLARGE THE FACTORY.

⑥ **VITAMINS** HELP TO RELEASE THE ENERGY FROM FATS, PROTEINS, AND CARBOHYDRATES.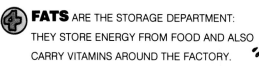

⑦ **MINERALS** ARE THE CARPENTERS — THEY HELP TO BUILD BONES AND TEETH.

⑧ WHEN ALL FOOD IS COMPLETELY DIGESTED, WHATEVER ISN'T USED OR STORED LEAVES THE FACTORY AS **WASTE**.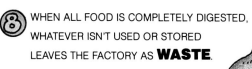

THE MICRONUTRIENTS

Proteins, carbohydrates, and fats are the three major nutrients that we need to get from the foods we eat. All three can be used by the body to provide the energy we need to do all the things we do—like sleeping, eating, reading a book, or running a race. They are also used as building materials for the many parts that make up our bodies.

We need fairly large amounts of proteins, carbohydrates, and fats each day. That's why they are called *macronutrients*. (*Macro-* means "big.") But they are not the only nutrients we need to be healthy.

We need small amounts of *micronutrients* as well—vitamins and minerals. Micronutrients aren't used for energy in the body, but they have very important jobs to do in helping to keep us healthy.

Water has no energy value, but it, too, is an important nutrient. We get some of the water we need by drinking it, but many foods also supply a lot of water. And, in fact, your own body is about two-thirds water.

Most Americans, except the very poor, get enough of the macronutrients. But because many people don't always eat the right kinds of foods, some of them may not be getting enough of the micronutrients in their diet. Others take vitamin and mineral supplements because of all the good things they've heard vitamins and minerals can do.

If you don't get enough vitamins or minerals, important chemical reactions in your body can't go on. Then you may get sick. But taking in too much of a vitamin or mineral may have bad effects, too. Choosing foods that supply the right amounts of the vitamins and minerals you need is an important part of eating a balanced diet.

WHAT ARE VITAMINS?

Almost everybody has heard of vitamins, but most people are not too sure about what a vitamin is.

Vitamins are chemicals that our bodies need and, in most cases, cannot make for themselves. Most vitamins are made by plants, and animals get them by eating plants and other animals.

The Two Groups of Vitamins

Vitamins are divided into two main groups, those that dissolve in water (*water soluble*) and those that dissolve only in fats or oils (*fat soluble*). The body stores fat-soluble vitamins in the liver and in the body fat. Because they can be stored in the body, we don't need to eat fat-soluble vitamins every day. But most water-soluble vitamins are not stored in the body in any large amounts, so we need to get a daily supply in the foods that we eat.

There are four fat-soluble vitamins: A, D, E, and K. The other nine vitamins are water soluble. They are vitamin C and eight B vitamins: thiamine (B-1), riboflavin (B-2), niacin (B-3), pantothenic acid (B-5), pyridoxine (B-6), folacin, cobalamin (B-12), and biotin.

What happened to the missing letters?

You may be wondering what happened to vitamins F, G, H, and I. And why are there so many extra Bs?

None of the vitamins are really missing. The first ones that were discovered were named in alphabetical order. (The chemical names came later, when scientists found out more about them.) The Danish researcher who discovered vitamin K named it after the Danish word for clotting, *Koagulation*, because vitamin K helps the blood to clot. Meanwhile, scientists had found that what they thought was a single vitamin B was really a group of vitamins that are usually found together in the same foods. So numbers were attached to the B. By the time the last B vitamins were discovered, the system of letter naming was out of style; thus, some of the B vitamins are called only by their chemical names.

What Do Vitamins Do?

Vitamins are not used by the body for energy, nor do they become parts of body structures. Most of them work together with enzymes (body proteins that help other chemicals to react). Some vitamin and enzyme partners help turn fat and carbohydrates into energy; others help to form body parts such as bones, body tissues, blood cells, and the body's genes. Some vitamins help in forming the body's defenses against disease-causing bacteria and viruses.

Vitamin C in action

Cut pieces of fruit turn brown when they are left out for a while. The brown color is formed when oxygen in the air reacts with chemicals in the fruit. Vitamin C protects foods from the action of oxygen.

Crush a chewable vitamin C tablet and dissolve it in ½ cup of water in a small bowl. In two other bowls place: ½ cup of lemon juice; ½ cup of plain water.

Now cut an apple into quarters. Wet one quarter thoroughly with the vitamin C solution. Wet another apple quarter with lemon juice, and the third with water. Let all four apple quarters stand at room temperature for an hour. Which ones turn brown? (Hint: Lemon juice contains vitamin C.)

Where Do We Get Vitamins?

A balanced diet can normally supply all the vitamins people need. Our bodies can make three vitamins (vitamins A and D and niacin) from other chemicals. (Carotene, the pigment that gives carrots their orange color, can be converted to vitamin A, for example.) Bacteria in our intestines may also help make some vitamins.

Some people take vitamin supplements that are either natural substances produced from foods, or synthetic chemicals made in factories. Vitamins may also be added to certain foods. Vitamin D, for example, is commonly added to milk. Baked goods made with "enriched" flours contain vitamins added to replace those that were lost during processing.

Our Vitamin Needs

The total amount of vitamins that we need is very small— only milligrams or micrograms of each one per day. (A milligram is about the size of a crystal of sugar or salt; a microgram is one-thousandth of a milligram, or 0.000000035 ounce.) An ounce of vitamin B-12 would provide the daily requirement for more than nine million

people! All the vitamins a person needs each day add up to about an eighth of a teaspoon.

Sometimes one form of a vitamin is stronger than another. A smaller amount of a stronger form can do as much as a larger amount of a weaker form. In addition, some forms are more easily used by the body, so that more of the vitamin can actually work.

Many of the vitamins may be chemically changed by heat or light, so shipping or cooking foods or storing a bottle of vitamin pills on the shelf may cause the vitamins to lose some of their strength.

Labels on food packages or vitamin supplements often list the amount of vitamins in products as a percentage of the *U.S. RDA*. These letters stand for "United States Recommended Daily Allowance," a rough estimate of the amount of each nutrient the average person should get each day to stay healthy. The U.S. RDA is based on the *RDA*, or "Recommended Dietary Allowance," established for each essential nutrient by health experts at the National Research Council of the National Academy of Sciences. The

RDA for each nutrient is not just one number but a whole table of values depending on a person's age and sex. But even the RDAs are just averages and do not fit everyone, all the time. (You may need more vitamins than usual when you are sick, for example.)

Vitamins Work All Over the Body

Some vitamins are known for their effects on certain parts of the body. Even though vitamin A is the vitamin that keeps the skin from getting rough, it doesn't work only in skin cells. Rough skin is just one of the first signs that a person is not getting enough vitamin A. Most vitamins work in nearly all body cells. When people do not eat a well-balanced diet, they may not get enough of certain vitamins, and illnesses might occur. These *deficiency diseases* can often be cured simply by taking the vitamin that is missing.

Did you know . . .

Some foods contain *antivitamins*, chemicals that prevent vitamins from working in the body. Some kinds of fish, for example, contain the enzyme thiaminase, which breaks down thiamine into forms the body can't use. Heat destroys the enzyme, so when fish is cooked, its thiamine can be used by the body. But when people eat raw fish, the thiamine can't be used.

THE VITAMIN PIONEERS

Vitamins were discovered when doctors and scientists tried to figure out what was causing various diseases. For centuries the experts were puzzled, but in this century all the pieces of the puzzle came together.

A Mystery Disease

Beriberi is a disease that affects the heart and nervous system and can cause paralysis and death. (Its name means "I can't, I can't!"—a good way to describe how tired and weak people feel when they are suffering from beriberi.) It was a problem in China for nearly 4,500 years. In the late 1800s more than 1,000 Japanese sailors were dying from it each year.

One piece to the puzzle was uncovered when a 19th-century Japanese navy doctor found that only the sailors who ate the standard navy diet of white rice got sick. Sailors who ate supplies of foods including vegetables, fish, bread, and milk did not get beriberi. About ten years later, a Dutch doctor found that white rice did indeed seem to be the culprit.

Vital Nutrients

In 1911 a Polish chemist, Casimir Funk, discovered which nutrient was missing in white rice. With just a milligram of this substance he cured a pigeon paralyzed by beriberi. The mystery nutrient was a chemical in the amine family. Funk suggested that there was a whole group of chemicals in foods that prevented various diseases when they were eaten in small amounts. He named them *vitamines*. (*Vita* means "life," so "vitamines" are amines needed for life.) In 1926 the substance discovered by Casimir Funk was identified as thiamine. But as more "vitamines" were identified, it was found that most of them aren't amines. So scientists dropped the "e" and called them *vitamins*.

I CAN'T! I CAN'T!

WHAT ARE MINERALS?

The world is made up of tiny building blocks called *atoms*. There are more than 100 different kinds of atoms, and each one has its own unique properties. An *element* is a substance that contains only one type of atom. There are more than 100 elements.

Our bodies contain close to 40 elements, and 60 elements have been found in various life forms. However, just four elements—carbon, hydrogen, oxygen, and nitrogen—make up 96 percent of the body's weight! The other elements besides these four are called minerals.

If you weigh 62 pounds, all of the minerals in your body weigh less than 2½ pounds! Although minerals make up a relatively small portion of the body, they play very important roles.

Major Minerals and Trace Minerals

Our bodies contain larger amounts of some minerals than of others. Calcium alone makes up half of the total 2½ pounds of minerals in the body. Calcium and six others (phosphorus, sulfur, potassium, sodium, chloride, and magnesium) together make up more than 99 percent of the weight of the body's minerals. These seven are called *macrominerals* or *major minerals* because they are present in the body in larger amounts than the others, and we need to eat larger amounts of them in our foods.

All the rest of the minerals combined make up only 0.01 percent of the body's weight! These other minerals—iron, zinc, copper, iodine, manganese, fluorine, chromium, cobalt, selenium, and molybdenum—are called *microminerals, trace minerals*, or *trace elements* because they are needed in much smaller amounts. The recommended dietary allowance of the major mineral calcium, for example, is 30,000 times as much as the RDA for the trace mineral selenium.

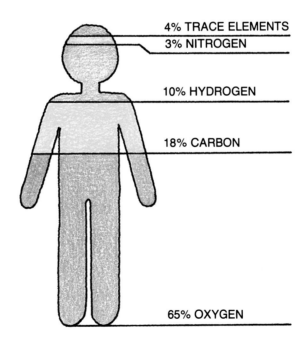

4% TRACE ELEMENTS
3% NITROGEN
10% HYDROGEN
18% CARBON
65% OXYGEN

What Do Minerals Do?

Minerals are used as building materials in body tissues, including the bones, blood, and teeth. They also help to regulate such body processes as blood clotting, the heartbeat, and the passage of messages along our nerves. Minerals help keep the fluids in our bodies at the right pressure and the right balance. They help the blood carry oxygen to

A salty taste

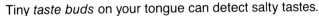

Tiny *taste buds* on your tongue can detect salty tastes.

Measure 8 ounces of water into a glass and stir in 1 teaspoon of salt until it dissolves. Now place a drop of the salt solution on the tip of your tongue. Rinse your mouth with clear water and place a drop of salt solution on the middle of your tongue. Try other drops on the left side, the right side, and near the back of your tongue, rinsing between each test. Which drops tasted salty? Try the same test with potassium chloride salt substitute. Does it have a salty taste, too?

Did you know . . .

Salt is the second most common ingredient that manufacturers add to foods (sugar is the first). Salt is added to flavor and preserve foods. Look for other common sodium sources on package labels:

baking powder
monosodium glutamate
sodium benzoate
sodium caseinate
sodium citrate

sodium nitrate
sodium phosphate
sodium propionate
sodium saccharin

all the body cells and help the cells get rid of their carbon dioxide waste products. Minerals are also important parts of enzymes and hormones involved in the work of the nerves and muscles.

The minerals in our bodies must be balanced. We can't have too much or too little, or problems can develop. A trace element can be just as important as a major mineral.

The trace elements are needed in very tiny amounts, but relatively large amounts can be poisonous or even deadly.

Getting Minerals from Foods

The leaves and seeds of plants are good sources of minerals, and animal products can be good sources, too. Our ancestors ate nearly every part of the animals they hunted or raised. Most people today don't eat bones (which are high in calcium and phosphorus) or the mineral-rich organ meats such as heart, kidney, and liver. The meats we eat are mainly muscle tissue (a good source for iron and copper). Dairy products supply calcium and phosphorus.

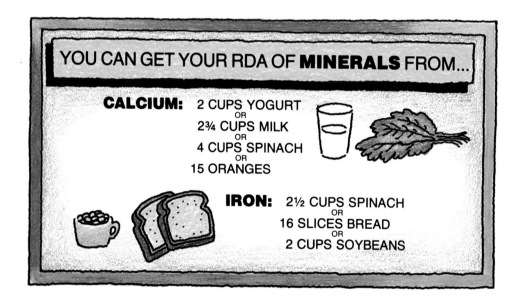

YOU CAN GET YOUR RDA OF **MINERALS** FROM...

CALCIUM: 2 CUPS YOGURT
OR
2¾ CUPS MILK
OR
4 CUPS SPINACH
OR
15 ORANGES

IRON: 2½ CUPS SPINACH
OR
16 SLICES BREAD
OR
2 CUPS SOYBEANS

Did you know . . .

Unlike calcium, which is constantly being added and taken away, once fluoride is in our bones it stays there. This mineral makes tooth enamel (the outer coating) stronger and more able to prevent damage by the acids produced by bacteria. People who drink water high in fluorides have less tooth decay. In many communities fluoride is added to drinking water. Dentists may also apply a fluoride coating to protect children's teeth.

Did you know . . .

A radioactive form of iodine is one of the dangerous elements in the fallout from a nuclear explosion. It is absorbed by the thyroid gland just like regular, nonradioactive iodine, and it can cause cancer. But iodine supplements can protect people from these harmful effects.

We also can get some minerals from nonfood sources, such as iron from foods cooked in an iron skillet.

Minerals are not absorbed very well by the body. For example, only 5 percent of the manganese, 10 percent of the iron, 10–20 percent of the zinc, and 30–50 percent of the calcium in the foods we eat are actually absorbed and used. (The rest pass out with the body wastes.) When supplies of a particular mineral are low, the body can compensate by absorbing more of it than usual.

VITAMINS AND MINERALS FOR GOOD HEALTH

Most doctors advise that a well-balanced diet will supply all of the nutrients that we need to be healthy. (A balanced diet is one in which you get enough of a variety of foods.) When you eat well, no additional supplements are necessary.

But not everyone eats a balanced diet. In many parts of the world, people do not get enough food to eat. They don't get enough nutrients to grow and be healthy. Others may get enough calories—in proteins, carbohydrates, and fats—but important micronutrients are missing in their diet. In some areas, for example, people eat mostly refined rice, or foods made from corn, and their diet lacks key vitamins. In some regions the diet is missing important minerals because the soil in which the food grows doesn't have enough of these minerals.

Maybe someone you know lives on junk food—sodas, chips, and doughnuts, for example. Most Americans don't eat that badly, but they do eat much less fresh fruits and vegetables, whole grains, and dairy products than our ancestors did in the past. So many people are barely getting enough of some nutrients, even though they may get "enough" to eat. Deficiency diseases are rare in Amer-

BALANCED DIET

JUNK FOOD DIET

ica today, which means most people are getting at least the minimum amounts of vitamins and minerals that they need. But because of poor eating habits, some people may not be as healthy as they could be.

Meanwhile, some people are getting too much of some vitamins or minerals. They take supplements that they think will give them energy, prevent colds, or keep them from aging.

Who needs vitamin and mineral supplements?

Doctors may prescribe supplements for people with special needs:

infants, pregnant and nursing women, growing children;
smokers and heavy drinkers;
women who take oral contraceptives;
people who take antacids, or certain drugs for diabetes, high blood pressure, malaria, or tuberculosis;
people with illnesses such as cancer or infections;
people who have had surgery (extra nutrients are needed for healing);
elderly people, who may need larger doses of vitamins because they cannot absorb them as well as they used to;
people who are dieting and may not be getting enough nutrients;
people living in areas where soils are deficient in certain nutrients;
vegetarians, who may not get enough of certain micro-nutrients, found mainly in animal products.

Vitamins and Minerals Work with Other Nutrients

Each nutrient has its own functions in the body, but nutrients work together. The body needs all of them, in the right amounts, to function properly.

Vitamin C, for example, helps increase the amount of iron the body absorbs. A glass of orange juice can double

the amount of iron absorbed from eggs and toast, and canned tomatoes in a rice casserole can increase the iron absorbed from the rice. Vitamin D helps calcium and phosphorus to be absorbed. Protein increases the absorption of zinc, and fats carry fat-soluble vitamins into the body.

Normally the nutrients work together, but when they are not in the right balance, they can interfere with each other. Too much vitamin C or zinc, for example, can prevent the body from using copper. Large amounts of protein reduce the amount of calcium the body can use.

Because vitamins work with other nutrients, the best way to get them is by eating a diet with varied foods at each meal. Vitamin supplements are best taken with a meal for this same reason. In addition, the body may be able to absorb and use them better while foods are being digested and absorbed.

Did you know . . .

Nutrients can also interact with drugs. Antacids, for example, contain a lot of aluminum, which can decrease the absorption of phosphorus and fluoride. Laxatives can cause a loss of calcium, potassium, fat, and fat-soluble vitamins. Aspirin causes small losses of blood (together with the iron it contains) in the digestive tract and can also interfere with the use of folacin. The calcium in milk binds the antibiotic tetracycline and blocks its absorption, but foods can aid the absorption of another antibiotic, erythromycin.

Getting the Best Nutrient
Value from Foods

There may be a big difference between the amount of a vitamin or mineral naturally found in a food and the amount of that nutrient you actually get when you eat it. Most people today don't eat fruits and vegetables right off the plant or drink milk straight out of the cow. Foods are shipped from farm to market—sometimes halfway around the world. They sit for days, weeks, or months in storage. Foods are processed in various ways to get them ready for people to buy, and then we cook them, peel them, or prepare them in other ways for eating.

At each stage of the long trip from the farm to your mouth, nutrients in the foods may be lost or changed. Some changes improve them, but in many cases food value is lost. For example, nutrients are lost when grains are milled or vegetables are peeled. Many water-soluble vitamins and minerals are lost during washing and when foods are cooked in water. Chemical reactions during storage can rob foods of vitamins.

To get more nutrients out of your food:

Eat whole-grain cereals, breads, and pastas.
Choose fresh or frozen foods rather than canned foods.
Store foods well wrapped to keep out air (leave fruits and vegetables like oranges and peas in their natural "wrappers" until use, and bake or boil potatoes in their skin to keep vitamins in).
Don't thaw or wash frozen vegetables before cooking.

Microwave cooking saves the most vitamins; pressure cooking and steaming are next best (you lose more than half the vitamin C by boiling vegetables).

Broil, fry, or roast meats to preserve B vitamins.

Use cooking water from vegetables and meat broth for soup and gravy.

Use juice or syrup from canned fruits in drinks or gelatin desserts.

Too much of a good thing can be harmful

Some people take vitamin or mineral supplements that supply very large doses dozens of times the RDA! Micronutrients in these "megadoses" may be helpful in a few, very special medical problems. But most experts believe that they aren't good for the average person, no matter what the ads promise.

Don't be worried, though, if you're getting a *little* more of some vitamins or minerals than you need. The foods you eat may supply two to three times the RDA of many nutrients. In most cases, this is OK.

But watch out for the fat-soluble vitamins A and D. Your body will store any amounts of these vitamins that it doesn't use. If you continue to get more than you need—in vitamin-fortified milk, cereal, and a multivitamin supplement, for example—your stored reserves may build up to harmful levels. Water-soluble vitamins are less likely to cause problems, because most of the excess passes out in your body wastes.

Sodium is the mineral most likely to be present in foods in too large amounts. People often take supplements of calcium, zinc, iron, iodine, magnesium, and selenium. Using potassium salt substitutes to cut down on sodium may result in a potassium overdose. Too much of any of these minerals can cause health problems.

WATER: THE FORGOTTEN NUTRIENT

Most people don't even think of water as a nutrient, but it is actually the most important one. There is more water inside us than any other substance. (The human body is between 55 and 85 percent water.) We can live without food for weeks or even months, but we wouldn't last more than two or three days without water. It is involved in nearly everything that goes on in our bodies.

What the Body's Water Does

Water carries things around in the body and into and out of cells. It brings the cells supplies of oxygen and nutrients and carries away carbon dioxide and other waste products. It also transports hormones, the body's chemical messengers, and enzymes, which help in chemical reactions.

Many reactions in the body can take place only in water. Water cushions and protects important body organs such as the brain, spinal cord, and lungs, and it lubricates the joints. It also helps to keep the body temperature normal.

Why We Need Water

Your body loses an average of 8 to 12 cups of water each day. About half of it leaves in the urine. You also lose water when you sweat and when you breathe. (Try breathing onto a cool mirror. The "fog" forms from water vapor in your breath.)

All the water we lose has to be replaced. When you feel thirsty, that is a signal that your water supplies are running low. Most people don't drink 8 cups of water each day. But we also get water from foods and drinks. Fruits and vegetables are 70 to 95 percent water, milk 87 percent, eggs 75 percent, meats 40 to 75 percent, cereals 8 to 20 percent, and crackers are 5 percent water.

Remember that water, vitamins, and minerals are just some of the nutrients your body needs. By choosing foods that supply them, you can help keep your body strong and healthy.

THE TWO GROUPS OF VITAMINS

WATER-SOLUBLE VITAMINS

Vitamin	What Does It Do?	Where Is It Found?
VITAMIN B-1 (Thiamine)	1. Helps body get energy from carbohydrates 2. Helps keep nervous system healthy	Dairy, eggs, ham, legumes, meat, whole grain and enriched bread, cereal, and pasta
VITAMIN B-2 (Riboflavin)	1. Helps body get energy from protein, fat, and carbohydrates 2. Helps keep skin, mucous membranes (like the lining in your nose), eyes, and nervous system healthy	Cheese, eggs, enriched grain products, leafy vegetables, liver, meat, milk, yeast, yogurt, produced by bacteria in intestines
VITAMIN B-3 (Niacin)	1. Helps body get energy from fats, carbohydrates, and protein 2. Helps keep skin, tongue, and digestive system healthy	Fish, leafy vegetables, legumes, meat, peanuts, poultry, sunflower seeds, whole or enriched grain products, yeast
VITAMIN B-5 (Pantothenic Acid)	1. Helps body turn food into energy 2. Helps form important body substances such as fatty acids, cholesterol, steroids, hemoglobin, antibodies, and nerve-regulating chemicals	Broccoli, dairy, eggs, fish, fruits, liver, meat, potatoes, poultry

RDA	Deficiency Symptoms	Danger of Overdose
1.0 mg for 7–10 yr. olds	Beriberi: nerve disorders, heart disorders, weak muscles	Not known, but too much of one B vitamin could cause deficiency of others
1.2 mg for 7–10 yr. olds	Scaly skin, cracked lips, sore, swollen red tongue	None known (See Thiamine)
13 mg NE* for 7–10 yr. olds	Pellagra: The 4 D's— dermatitis (skin inflammation), diarrhea, dementia (mental illness), death	Flushing of face and hands, liver problems, ulcers
Not established; 4–7 mg suggested	Deficiency is rare. Nervous disorders; tiredness; weight loss; burning feeling in feet; nausea	Diarrhea, water retention

* NE stands for "Niacin Equivalents"

Vitamin	What Does It Do?	Where Is It Found?
VITAMIN B-6 (Pyridoxine)	1. Helps body use proteins 2. Helps body make red blood cells 3. Helps body break down fats 4. Helps keep nervous system healthy 5. Helps form antibodies	Bananas, beans, eggs, fish, liver, meat, potato, whole grain products and enriched cereals
FOLACIN (Folate, Folic Acid)	1. Helps body form DNA and RNA and red blood cells 2. Helps body use proteins	Broccoli, grains, green leafy vegetables, liver, legumes, nuts, orange juice, peanuts, yeast
VITAMIN B-12 (Cobalamin)	1. Helps body form DNA and RNA and red blood cells 2. Helps body break down and use fat and protein 3. Helps keep nervous system healthy	Dairy, eggs, fish, meat, poultry. Not found in plant foods (also made by intestinal bacteria)
BIOTIN	1. Helps body get energy from carbohydrates 2. Helps body form amino acids and fatty acids	Cauliflower, cereals, dairy, eggs, kidney, legumes, liver, nuts, yeast
VITAMIN C (Ascorbic Acid)	1. Helps hold body cells together 2. Keeps gums healthy 3. Helps tooth and bone formation 4. Helps heal wounds 5. Helps form hormones and brain chemicals 6. Helps body absorb iron 7. Helps protect other vitamins from oxidation	Broccoli, cantaloupes, cauliflower, citrus fruits, peppers, potatoes, strawberries, tomatoes

RDA	Deficiency Symptoms	Danger of Overdose
1.4 mg for 7–10 yr. olds	Nerve disorders; muscular disorders	Headache, loss of coordination, muscle pain
100 mcg for 7–10 yr. olds	Blood disorder (anemia); weakness; diarrhea	None known, but may hide a deficiency of B-12
1.4 mcg for 7–10 yr. olds	Blood disorder; nervous system disorder	None known
Not established; 30–100 mcg suggested	Skin inflammation; depression; muscle pain	None known
45 mg for 7–10 yr. olds	Scurvy: loose teeth, bleeding gums, joint pain; lowered immunity	May develop a dependence on high dose; diarrhea; kidney and bladder stones; can cause a vitamin B-12 deficiency

FAT-SOLUBLE VITAMINS

Vitamin	What Does It Do?	Where Is It Found?
VITAMIN A (Retinol)	1. Needed for healthy eyes, skin, hair, and lining of throat and digestive system 2. Needed for growth of teeth and bones 3. Needed for reproduction 4. Helps keep immune system healthy	Broccoli, butter, cantaloupe, carrots, dairy, eggs, liver, spinach, sweet potatoes (plant foods contain beta-carotene, which the body changes into retinol)
VITAMIN D (Calciferol)	1. Helps the body absorb and use calcium and phosphorus for healthy bones and teeth 2. Helps maintain balance of calcium and phosphorus in blood for normal functions of muscle and nerves	Butter, eggs, fish liver oils, margarine, milk (also made in skin exposed to sunlight)
VITAMIN E (Tocopherol)	1. Helps the body make tissues like muscles, and red blood cells 2. Helps prevent damage to cell membranes, red blood cells, and other body tissue such as the lungs 3. Protects vitamin A and fatty acids from oxidation 4. Needed for reproduction	Eggs, fish, leafy vegetables, legumes, nuts, peanuts, vegetable oils, whole grain bread and cereals, and wheat germ
VITAMIN K	1. Helps blood to clot normally 2. Helps keep bones healthy	Cabbage, cauliflower, cereals, dairy, eggs, green leafy vegetables, liver, meats, peas, tea

RDA	Deficiency Symptoms	Danger of Overdose
700 mcg RE* for 7–10 yr. olds	Night blindness; blindness; scaly skin; lowered immunity	Dry skin, swelling, nausea, headache, diarrhea, weakened bones, liver and kidney damage, brain injury
10 mcg (400 IU)* for 7–10 yr. olds	Rickets in children (poor tooth and bone formation), softening of bone and teeth in adults	Stunted growth, loss of appetite, nausea, high blood pressure, kidney stones, calcium deposits
7 mg TE* for 7–10 yr. olds	Anemia, neurological problems	Too much E may prevent vitamin A and K from being used properly; headache, tiredness
30 mcg for 7–10 yr. olds	It takes longer than normal for blood to clot when bleeding occurs	Anemia, jaundice

* RE stands for "retinol equivalents"; IU stands for "International Units"; TE stands for "Tocopherol Equivalents".

MINERALS: MAJOR AND MINOR

MAJOR MINERALS

Mineral	What Does It Do?	Where Is It Found?
CALCIUM (Ca)	1. Helps build bones and teeth 2. Helps blood clot 3. Helps muscles contract 4. Helps nerves send messages 5. Helps keep cell membranes healthy	Citrus fruits, dairy, dark green vegetables, legumes, salmon, sardines, shellfish, tofu
PHOSPHORUS (P)	1. Helps build bones and teeth 2. Helps body get energy from food 3. Helps form cell membranes, enzymes, and genes 4. Important for acid-base balance 5. Helps in work of muscles, nerves	Dairy, eggs, fish, legumes, meat, nuts, poultry, soft drinks, whole grain breads and cereals
POTASSIUM (K)	1. Helps maintain normal acid-base balance and water balance in cells 2. Needed for normal work of muscles, heart, and nerves 3. Helps body get energy from food	Cocoa, fruits (esp. bananas, oranges), legumes, meat, peanut butter, potatoes, vegetables, whole grain breads and cereals
SULFUR (S)	1. Part of protein in every cell 2. Part of hair, nails, skin, cartilage, tendons	Clams, dairy, eggs, fish, legumes, meat, nuts, peanuts, wheat germ

RDA	Deficiency Symptoms	Danger of Overdose
800 mg for 7–10 yr. olds	Children: rickets (stunted bone growth). Adults: osteoporosis (loss of bone, bones fracture more easily)	Calcium deposits, decreases absorption of other minerals like iron and zinc
800 mg for 7–10 yr. olds	Weakness, loss of bone; deficiency can be caused by antacids	May create calcium deficiency, causing bone loss
None set. 1,600–2,000 mg minimum	Weakness, paralysis, abnormal heart rhythm, kidney and lung problems	Paralysis, heart attack
None set. Supplied by sulfur-containing proteins	Related to protein deficiency	Stunted growth, liver damage

Mineral	What Does It Do?	Where Is It Found?
SODIUM (Na)	1. Regulates water and acid-base balances 2. Needed for healthy muscles and nerves 3. Needed to produce energy	Table salt; most foods have some sodium
CHLORIDE (Cl)	1. Needed for acid-base and fluid balances 2. Part of stomach digestive acid 3. Activates enzyme in saliva	Table salt, almost all foods except fruit
MAGNESIUM (Mg)	1. Helps nerves and muscles work properly 2. Helps build bones and teeth 3. Helps make proteins 4. Helps body adjust to cold 5. Part of more than 300 enzymes	Dairy, fish, green leafy vegetables, legumes, nuts, peanut butter, seeds, tofu, whole grain bread and cereal
FLUORIDE (F)	1. Helps build strong teeth and bones	Drinking water, rice, seafood, soybeans, spinach, tea, toothpastes
CHROMIUM (Cr)	1. Helps body use carbohydrates 2. Works with vitamin E	Dairy, dark green leafy vegetables, legumes, liver, meat, peanuts, whole grain bread and cereal, yeast
SELENIUM (Se)	1. Helps prevent breakdown of fats and other body chemicals 2. Works with vitamin E	Dairy, eggs, garlic, meat, poultry, seafood, whole grain bread and cereal

RDA	Deficiency Symptoms	Danger of Overdose
None set. 400–500 mg minimum. 1–3 g safe for adults	Loss of appetite, muscle cramps	High blood pressure for some people
None set. 600–750 mg minimum	Loss of appetite, muscle cramps, poor growth	Vomiting, upsets acid-base balance
170 mg for 7–10 yr. olds	Weakness, irregular heartbeat, spasms, neurological problems	Neurological problems, diarrhea, upsets calcium-magnesium balance (excess magnesium is stored in bones)
1.5–2.5 mg for 7–10 yr. olds	More chance of tooth decay	Spotted teeth and bones; in large doses, death possible
50–200 mcg for 7–10 yr. olds	Unable to use glucose properly (diabetes)	None known. (Workers exposed to chromium dust may suffer lung and skin damage)
30 mcg for 7–10 yr. olds	Heart and muscle damage, higher chance of cancer and high blood pressure	Hair and nail loss, digestive disorders

Mineral	What Does It Do?	Where Is It Found?
MOLYBDENUM (Mb)	1. Part of enzymes 2. Helps turn wastes into urine 3. Helps get energy from food 4. Helps body use iron	Legumes, green leafy vegetables, liver, whole grain bread and cereal

TRACE OR MINOR MINERALS

Mineral	What Does It Do?	Where Is It Found?
IRON (Fe)	1. Helps build red blood cells 2. Part of enzymes and proteins 3. Helps body get energy	Dark leafy vegetables, eggs, legumes, liver, meat, nuts, seeds, whole and enriched bread and cereal
COPPER (Cu)	1. Helps build red blood cells and bones 2. Helps keep blood vessels and nerves healthy 3. Part of enzymes	Liver, seafood, legumes, raisins, cocoa, nuts, potatoes, whole grain bread and cereal
ZINC (Zn)	1. Part of nearly 100 enzymes 2. Needed for normal growth 3. Helps wounds heal 4. Needed for taste and appetite	Dairy, eggs, fish, liver, meat, poultry, seafood, whole grain bread and cereal
MANGANESE (Mn)	1. Part of enzymes 2. Helps bones grow 3. Helps keep brain, nerves, and muscles healthy 4. Needed for reproduction	Cocoa, fruits, legumes, nuts, tea, vegetables, whole grain bread and cereal
IODINE (I)	1. Part of thyroid hormones 2. Needed for normal reproduction	Dairy products, iodized salt, seafood, sea salt, vegetables

(40

RDA	Deficiency Symptoms	Danger of Overdose
50–150 mcg for 7–10 yr. olds	Not known. (In animals: loss of weight, shortened life span)	Use of copper, cobalt, and enzymes disrupted, producing stiff, swollen joints
10 mg for 7–10 yr. olds	Anemia, tiredness, shortness of breath, lowered immunity	Heart, liver and pancreas damage, shock, death
1–2 mg for 7–10 yr. olds	Anemia; damage to bone, nervous system, lungs, and arteries; may be linked to high cholesterol, which increases heart disease risk	Nausea, vomiting, diarrhea, liver damage
10 mg for 7–10 yr. olds	Poor growth, failure to mature sexually, lowered immunity, loss of appetite, less sense of taste, scaly skin	Nausea, vomiting, diarrhea, anemia, fever, can cause copper deficiency
2–3 mg for 7–10 yr. olds	Not known. (In animals: poor growth, birth defects, abnormal bone growth)	Nervous system disorder
120 mcg for 7–10 yr. olds	Goiter (enlarged thyroid gland)	Goiter, heart problems, cretinism (mental and physical retardation)

NUTRITIONAL VALUES OF COMMON FOODS

Food	Portion size		Vit. A (IU)	B-1 (mg)	B-2 (mg)	Niacin (mg)
Applesauce (sweetened)	1	cup	28	.04	.08	.4
Bacon	3	pieces	0	.13	.05	1.4
Banana	1	banana	92	.05	.11	0.6
Broccoli (raw)	1	cup	1356	.06	.10	0.6
Butter	1	tablespoon	918	.00	.01	0.0
Cake (devil's food)	1	piece	47	.06	.08	.8
Cod (baked w/ butter)	3½	ounces	90	.08	.08	3.0
Corn (cooked on cob)	1	ear	167	.17	.06	1.2
Cornflakes	1¼	cups	1250	.40	.40	5.0
Eggs (boiled)	1	large	260	.04	.15	0.0
French fries	10	fries	0	.06	.02	1.2
Green beans (boiled)	½	cup	413	.05	.06	.4
Hamburger (broiled)	3½	ounces	3	.04	.21	6.5
Hot dog (beef)	1	frank	0	.03	.06	1.4
Milk (whole)	1	cup	307	.09	.40	.2
Milkshake (chocolate)	1	cup	258	.14	.67	.4
Orange juice	1	cup	500	.22	.07	1.0
Peanut butter	1	tablespoon	0	.02	.02	2.2
Peas (boiled)	½	cup	478	.21	.12	1.6
Potato (baked w/ skin)	1	potato	0	.22	.07	3.3
Spaghetti	1	cup	0	.20	.11	1.5
Steak (sirloin)	3	ounces	18	.10	.23	3.3
Toast (white bread)	1	slice	0	.03	.08	0.9
Tomato sauce	½	cup	2399	.16	.14	2.8
Turkey (light meat)	3½	ounces	0	.06	.13	6.8

B-6 (mg)	B-12 (mcg)	C (mg)	Ca (mg)	P (mg)	Na (mg)	Fe (mg)	Mg (mg)	Cu (mg)	Zn (mg)
.06	.00	4	10	18	8	.90	8	.11	.10
.05	.33	6	2	64	303	.31	5	.032	.62
.66	.00	10	7	22	1	.35	33	.119	.19
.14	.00	82	42	58	24	.78	22	.040	.36
.00	.00	0	3	3	123	.03	0		.00
.03	.26	0	54	128	341	1.21	16	.101	.41
.40	2.00	0	24	220	224	.60	30	.025	.80
.18	.00	5	5	113	4	.86	40	.063	.87
.50	1.48	15	1	18	351	1.80	3	.019	.08
.06	.77	0	28	90	69	1.04	6		.72
.12	.00	6	4	43	15	.67	11	.082	.21
.04	.00	6	29	24	2	.79	16	.064	.23
.30	3.28	0	11	170	83	2.44	20	.082	5.18
.07	.87	14	11	50	585	.81	2	.030	1.24
.10	.87	0	291	228	120	.10	33		.90
.08	.95	7	396	378	333	.93	48	.034	1.44
.10	.00	124	42	72	12	2.20	54	.284	.34
.06	.00	0	5	60	65	.30	25	.094	.50
.17	.00	11	22	94	2	1.24	31	.138	.95
.70	.00	26	20	115	16	2.75	55	.616	.65
.01	.00	0	11	70	1	2.25	25	.028	.70
.29	2.77	0	11	218	63	3.01	28	.137	5.75
.01	.00	0	30	26	123	.68	5	.033	.15
.33	.00	32	17	39	738	.94	23	.239	.30
.54	.37	0	21	208	63	1.41	26	.048	2.04

GLOSSARY

antivitamins—chemicals that prevent vitamins from working in the body.

ascorbic acid—vitamin C.

beriberi—a deficiency disease due to lack of vitamin B-1.

biotin—a B vitamin.

calciferol—vitamin D.

cobalamin—vitamin B-12.

deficiency diseases—illnesses caused by a lack of essential nutrients.

element—a substance containing only one type of building
blocks (atoms).

fat-soluble vitamins—those able to dissolve in fats (A, D,
E, and K).

folacin—a B vitamin; also called folic acid.

macrominerals or *major minerals*—minerals needed in
large amounts (calcium, phosphorus, sulfur, potassium, sodium, chloride, and magnesium).

macronutrients—nutrients needed in large amounts (proteins, carbohydrates, and fats).

microminerals—trace elements; minerals needed in very
small amounts.

micronutrients—nutrients needed in small amounts (vitamins and minerals).

minerals—the elements besides carbon, hydrogen, oxygen, and nitrogen.

niacin—vitamin B-3.

nutrients—necessary food substances, such as vitamins and minerals.

pantothenic acid—vitamin B-5.

pyridoxine—vitamin B-6.

RDA (recommended dietary allowance)—the amount of a nutrient that experts say a person of a particular age, sex, and weight should eat each day.

retinol—vitamin A.

riboflavin—vitamin B-2.

thiamine—vitamin B-1.

tocopherol—vitamin E.

trace elements—minerals needed in very small amounts (iron, zinc, copper, iodine, manganese, fluorine, chromium, cobalt, selenium, and molybdenum).

U.S. RDA (the United States recommended daily allowance)—the amount of a nutrient needed each day for good health (a value suitable for most people, based on the RDA).

vitamins—nutrients that prevent deficiency diseases when eaten in very small amounts.

water-soluble vitamins—those able to dissolve in water (B vitamins and C).

FOR FURTHER READING

Cobb, Vicki. *More Science Experiments You Can Eat.* New York: Lippincott, 1979.

Cobb, Vicki. *Science Experiments You Can Eat.* New York: Lippincott, 1972.

O'Neill, Catherine. *How and Why: A Kid's Book About the Body.* Mount Vernon, N.Y.: Consumer Reports Books, 1988.

Ontario Science Center. *Foodworks.* Toronto: Kids Can Press, 1986.

Our Body: A Child's First Library of Learning. Alexandria, Va.: Time Life Books, 1988.

INDEX

Anemia, 33, 35, 41
Antacids, 24, 25, 37
Antibiotics, 25
Antivitamins, 13
Ascorbic acid, 8, 32
Aspirin, 25
Atoms, 16

Beriberi, 14, 15, 31
Biotin, 8, 32
Breads, 14, 26, 30, 34, 36, 38,
    40, 42–43

Calciferol, 34–35
Calcium, 16–18, 20, 21, 25, 27,
    36–37, 43
Carbohydrates, 6, 10, 22
Carotene, 11
Cereals, 26, 27, 29, 30, 32, 34,
    36, 38, 40
Chloride, 16–17, 38–39
Chromium, 17, 38–39
Cobalamin, 8, 32
Cobalt, 17
Copper, 17, 20, 25, 40–41, 43
Corn, 22, 42–43

Dairy products, 11, 14, 20, 22,
    25, 27, 29, 30, 32, 34, 36, 38,
    40, 42–43
Deficiency diseases, 13, 22–23,
    31, 33, 35, 37, 39, 41

Elements, 16
Enzymes, 10, 13, 19, 29

Fats, 6, 8, 10, 22, 25
Fat-soluble vitamins, 8, 25, 27,
    34–35
Fish, 13, 14, 30, 32, 34, 36, 38,
    40, 42–43
Fluoride, 21, 25, 38–39
Fluorine, 17
Folacin, 8, 25, 32–33
Fruits, 10, 22, 24–26, 29, 30,
    32, 36, 40, 42–43
Funk, Casimir, 15

Grains, 22, 26, 30, 32, 34, 36,
    38, 40

Hormones, 19, 29

Iodine, 17, 21, 27, 40–41
Iron, 17, 18, 20, 21, 24–25, 27,
    40–41, 43

Laxatives, 25
Legumes, 30, 32, 34, 36, 38, 40

Macrominerals, 16–17, 36–40
Macronutrients, 6, 7
Magnesium, 16–17, 27, 38–39,
    43
Major minerals, 16–17, 36–40

Manganese, 17, 21, 40–41
Meats, 29, 30, 32, 34, 36, 38, 40, 42–43
Microminerals, 17, 19–20, 40–41
Micronutrients, 6, 7, 22, 27
Minor minerals, 17, 19–20, 40–41
Molybdenum, 17, 40–41

Niacin, 8, 11, 30–31, 42
Nutritional values of common foods, 42–43
Nuts, 30, 32, 34, 36, 38, 40, 42–43

Osteoporosis, 37
Overdose, danger of, 31, 33, 35, 37, 39, 41

Pantothenic acid, 8, 30–31
Pellagra, 31
Phosphorus, 16–17, 20, 25, 36–37, 43
Potassium, 16–17, 25, 27, 36–37
Poultry, 30, 32, 36, 38, 40
Proteins, 6, 12, 22, 25
Pyridoxine, 8, 32, 43

RDA (Recommended Dietary Allowance), 12–13, 17, 27, 31, 33, 35, 37, 39, 41
Retinol, 34–35
Riboflavin, 8, 30–31
Rice, 14, 15, 22, 25, 38
Rickets, 35, 37

Salt, 19, 38
Scurvy, 15, 33

Seeds, 30, 38, 40
Selenium, 17, 27, 38–39
Sodium, 16–17, 19, 27, 38–39, 43
Sulfur, 16–17, 36–37

Thiaminase, 13
Thiamine, 8, 13, 15, 30–31
Tocopherol, 34–35
Trace elements, 17, 19–20, 40–41

USRDA (United States Recommended Daily Allowance), 12–13

Vegetables, 14, 22, 26, 29, 30, 32, 34, 36, 38, 40, 42–43
Vitamins
    A: 8, 11, 27, 34–35, 42
    B-1: 8, 13, 15, 30–31, 42
    B-2: 8, 30–31, 42
    B-3: 8, 11, 30–31, 42
    B-5: 8, 30–31
    B-6: 8, 32–33, 43
    B-12: 8, 11–12, 32–33, 43
    C: 8, 10, 11, 15, 24–25, 27, 32–33, 43
    D: 8, 11, 25, 27, 34–35
    E: 8, 34–35
    K: 8, 9, 34–35

Water, 6, 21, 28–29, 38
Water-soluble vitamins, 8, 26, 27, 30–33
Wheat germ, 34, 36

Yeast, 30, 32, 38

Zinc, 17, 21, 25, 27, 40–41, 43